I0141341

# Love Notes

# for

# Children

Wendy Vaughn

Eagle One Publishing

Escondido, CA

ISBN 978-0-692-12175-7

ISBN 978-0-692-12175-7

Copyright ©2018 by Wendy Vaughn

Published by Eagle One Publishing, 451 West El Norte Parkway, #303, Escondido, CA 92026

## Cover Design By Victoria Vinton

All rights reserved. No part of this book may be reproduced by any mechanical, photographic, or electronic process, or in the form of a phonographic recording, nor may it be stored in a retrieval system, transmitted, or otherwise be copied for public or private use—other than for "fair use" as brief quotations embodied in articles and reviews without prior written permission of the author.

The author of this book does not dispense medical advice or prescribe the use of any technique as a form of treatment for physical or medical problems without the advice of a physician, either directly or indirectly. The intent of the author is only to offer information of a general nature to help you in your quest for emotional and spiritual well-being.

In the event you use any of the information in this book for yourself, which is your constitutional right, the author and the publisher assume no responsibility for your actions.

Wendy's personal life experiences have allowed her to open her heart to children for whom she shares her counsel in this book.This book offers the reader the opportunity to expand their perspectives on numerous topics and gain emotional strength from the wisdom parted.

**B.P., Riverside, CA**

A must read book for children to enable, guide and direct them to be their best in life!

**C.B.Toledo**
**California State Retiree**

Wendy has a remarkable way of sharing her knowledge to help children understand, accept, and love themselves. Her book reinforces depth of life lessons for children to recognize and share their own needs, be kind to people and animals, stand up for their beliefs and share their love with others. She shows children that they are valued, have intuitive knowledge to trust their own judgment, and that their feelings matter. Children and their parents will find her book a lift to the reader's spirit, transformative, and a continuous guide to reread.

**Dr. Suki Stone**
**Creator/Founder You Read Program**

# Prologue

This book is an extension and updated version of my first book, *"For Children of the World With Love"*. My original intentions for FCOTWWL were to get basic concepts out into the world to help empower children. With everything that has transpired over recent years, I am now prompted to elaborate more on these lessons and to comment on events that have affected our world and have caused a lack of harmony and peace.

I hope to empower children, and help them acquire a sense of confidence so they can reach for the stars, achieve their goals, and pursue their dreams and wishes.

This book is intended for ages 10 years old and up.

It is meant to be read over and over as you grow and as you are able to understand and grasp each concept.

So children, please accept the following pages as *my love notes to you.*

I have incorporated vocabulary words into some topics to relay what their meanings represent or symbolize to me. They are not intended to be exact dictionary definitions.

The words I have selected are meant to display examples of the topics they either precede or follow to help emphasize the meaning behind these love notes.

These vocabulary  words are also significant because they will be there for you to lean on throughout your life.

# Introduction

After reading this book, may you come away with:

- ❖ feeling more empowered
- ❖ having more self-esteem
- ❖ believing in yourself with more confidence
- ❖ having the tools to help you through adulthood
- ❖ acknowledging we are all related spiritually
- ❖ knowing you are never alone in this world
- ❖ and having the awareness you are loved!

## Dedication

To

My Sister

Cynthia R. Vestal

(Cynde)

With Love And Appreciation

For Being

The Best Big Sister

I Could Have Ever Hoped For

And

For Setting An Example To Follow

Of A

Woman Having Courage And Grace

## Acknowledgments

With Love And Thanks For The Laughs

And Support


Bonnie Poulsen

Carla Wedge

Francine Berg

Kathy Cross

Lisa Sandler

Liz Caputa

Pamela Aldrete


And A Special Thank You And Appreciation To

Dr. Suki Stone

For Without Her Unconditional Love and Help

This Book Would Not Have Been Possible

# Contents

# COURAGE

# COURAGE

The word courage first brings to mind brave men and women who fight to defend our country while they serve in the military.

Courage represents a much **bigger** concept to me.

For example, courage can be you standing up to a bully at school or anytime a bully is in your face or in your way. It means being able to get up and face whatever struggle, disappointment, or whatever situation you find yourself in each and every day.

It means facing any problems with courage and using your courage to handle them.

You will find as you grow up there will be decisions you will have to face by reaching  within to find your courage.

Courage means not giving up during hard times. Courage means standing up for what you believe in even if it means you are standing alone in order to set a good example for others to do the right thing. Courage is believing in yourself and doing what is right at all times by listening to your conscience.

For example, when you witness other children in a crowd picking on an individual,  standing up to them in defiance to stop this action is acting with courage. By stopping others in their hurtful actions, you are expressing your courage to help change the bad behavior of others.

Courage will be there for you to draw upon your entire life. Courage means going through each day of your life with conviction and bravery.

Courage also means not being afraid to communicate and express your feelings when someone says or does something to hurt or offend you or when you witness them hurting others by their words or actions.

Courage can also mean standing up for yourself or for a topic or point of view when no one else has the conviction or courage to fight for it.

# Chapter 1

## Hold Onto The Power of Your Self-Worth

I need you to realize you have the power to change things in your environment and in our world for good. Your own individual age may be small in numbers but your ability **to make a difference** is huge!

For example, when I was growing up the adage of 'children need to be seen and not heard' was quoted quite often.  Honor your father and mother. All well and good, right?

For example, if your home environment is one where your parents scream at you constantly, or they raise their hands and hurt you or abuse you,

if that situation is truly the case, it must be brought

to someone other than your parents' attention so

that pattern is reported to the authorities in charge

so they can stop it from happening to you ever

again. Remember respect is *earned not owed.* If a

person mistreats me, I feel I don't owe them any

respect whatsoever and *neither* should you.

We hear on the news now that people are finally

coming forward with stories of abusive behavior

that was done to them years earlier in their lives.

For example, over 160 females, who competed for

the U.S. Olympics GymnasticTeam, testified

against their doctor who had molested them during

their physical examinations and treatment for

their injuries.

This is only one example of how these occurrences

can stop if you each hold your power. Use your own

voice to speak up *anytime* someone takes advantage

of their position of authority over you. Call the police

or tell a counselor or principal or people you can trust.

The above example may be one way where you have

to reach into the very core of your being to tap into

the courage you own to deal with issues like this one.

There may be parents in some families who don't

take the time to explain to their children, boys

or girls, that *no one* in any authority or role such as

a teacher, a doctor, a parent, an older family member, a coach, a priest, or rabbi – *no one* – has any right to inappropriately touch your private parts in *any* manner. If this happens to any one of you and the person doing this tells you to keep this secret or threatens to harm you, or anyone you love if you don't keep this secret is a *sure* sign they are doing something to you that they *shouldn't* be doing.

In a different example, each person needs to be aware of how they talk to others and how they treat other friends, classmates, or other people they interact with during the day. Your tone of voice can be uplifting or condescending. Be aware of how you present your discussions to or about your friends so that what you are trying to express is clearly understood

so that feelings aren't hurt or misunderstood.

Are you personally responsible for bullying someone?

Are you going out of your way to be mean or

disrespectful to another classmate or sibling or friend?

Is the tone of your voice condescending when you talk

to or about someone? Would others hearing you talk

about another person, think you also do not respect

them since you are talking about another individual in a

disrespectful tone and manner? Think before you act.

Make note that **no one** on this planet is any better than

you or anyone else. They are not superior over another

because of their religion, skin color, age, sexual

preference, country they come from, community they live in or any other circumstance. Remembering this fact will help you through the rest of your life.

Some people think poking fun at siblings or friends by putting them down in a joking manner is all right. It is *not!* They are trying to demean them and it can create a sense of inferiority in a person. Stop doing it before it ever begins.

Diversity is what makes America strong.
It is the very fabric of our country's founding principles.

We will talk about this further in an upcoming chapter.

## <u>RESPONSIBLE</u>

## Responsible

If someone describes themselves to me as being a responsible person, I can interpret they are telling me they are reliable, trustworthy, and dependable.

It can also represent that person is responsible for his or her own actions and that he or she accepts responsibility for every undertaking, action, or duty they complete.

In other words, being responsible means taking accountability for your own actions.

Taking ownership by acknowledging you did something

wrong, or you made a mistake is taking accountability and admitting responsibility for an action you took. Being able to be responsible and make things right when something doesn't turn out well is owning up to situations and correcting them.

It helps build character and it also shows that you can learn to be open for improvement and self-correction at all times.

## Chapter 2

## We Don't Have To Be Perfect

Sometimes we make mistakes in our lives.

Making mistakes helps us learn.

For example, you might put the wrong answer down on

a test. You might really mess up and don't know how

to fix something. Or make a much *bigger* mistake.

Whether big or small, we all make mistakes.

Without mistakes we wouldn't learn the correct way

to answer a problem. We wouldn't know a better

solution for ourselves *until* we made a wrong solution

or mistake *first*.

Mistakes will always be a part of growing up and will happen well into our adulthood. Sometimes we need a big mistake to happen before we can find our place in the world. Sometimes mistakes are a blessing in disguise. They also help to build character.

This is just a reminder for you not to be too hard on yourself when mistakes occur.

Being honest about your mistakes and facing them head on will help you to build your honest, truthful character and reach the integrity you will want to capture in life. I will comment further on this topic in the chapter on truth and integrity.

Special Quote Related To This Topic

By

Oprah Winfrey

"Failure is a great teacher, and,

if you are open to it,

every mistake has a lesson to offer."

# Chapter 3

## Learning To Take Time For Ourselves

As we grow up and develop through different stages, we become so busy with our studies and activities, we forget to take time for ourselves.

It's important to be able to spend time alone by ourselves for several reasons.

We need to have this quiet time so we can think, dream, and learn to be by ourselves.

Whether you come from a family with several siblings or whether you are an only child, time spent by yourself in solitude helps you to become better in touch with your own feelings.

Solitude gives you balance and a sense of knowing yourself. It will help you be free of anxiety during times you may find yourself alone for a period of time.

This special alone time helps us have the solitude we need so that we can develop a sense of well being about ourselves as we grow into adulthood.

Time alone helps us to do things by ourselves so we can learn to complete things without anyone else's help, such as a puzzle or drawing or project, reading a book and the action of completion adds to our own self-esteem.

We build confidence when we are by ourselves so that any future solitude we may face doesn't make us feel vulnerable later on when we are adults.

Taking time for our own solitude helps us to honor our 'child within' so that we can know what gives us happiness and gives us the time we need to reflect on our lives.

It helps us get to know what we love as children, what we like about ourselves, and what we love to remember about our childhood.

You will be a person who has a good balance in your life when you reach adulthood and have a partner or are in a marriage, and you can remember to take the time to be alone by yourself sometimes.

This will give you some breathing space so that you can do the things you enjoy doing by yourself without losing your own identity which is very important for you to always maintain.

As you grow into adulthood and you face more challenging problems, remember to take time out for yourself and watch a movie that will make you laugh and help you get back in touch with your 'child within'.

Special Quote Related To This Topic

By

Jerry Lewis

As

Professor Julius Kelp

In "The Nutty Professor"

*"You Might As Well Like Yourself.*

*Just Think About All The Time*

*You're Gonna Have To Spend With You."*

# Chapter 4

## Understanding Friends and Family

Relationships will always be a challenge in our lifetime. Harmonious relationships take patience, understanding, tolerance, and acceptance of our friends' and family's traits, talents, and shortcomings.

When we speak about our birthdays, we talk about our astrological sign and symbols and what the symbols represent as far as when our personalities are formed.

I find it uncanny that descriptions of personalities

born under various sun signs, as they are called, are

quite accurate.

Some books break our personalities down enough to

separate them as to how the sign relates to when we

are a child, or how the personalities are different

under the same sign for a man or woman as an adult,

or in the role of a boss, or the general personalities

of the sun sign itself.

I found such a book when I was growing up so I could

read and study my own personality traits. My solitude

time afforded me this luxury so that I could develop

an inner sense of acceptance and well-being about

myself – who I am, and what I am.

The book on sun signs also offered me the time to study my own family, and learn about each one of their individual strengths and weaknesses.

I was able to relate to my own strengths and weaknesses discussed in the book. I compared their traits with how I perceived my own.

This book helped me to better understand my family members similar connection as well as what made us unique.

It gave me a greater sense of appreciation of their abilities and talents, and not just because they were my family.

I also called in research when I met a new boy.
I wanted to see what his character traits were and
find out if we would be or not be compatible.

I hope this example gives you a reminder to take the
time to seek information about your friends and
family and learn about their traits and
personalities. You might want to start a conversation
and communicate with your family or friends; take
the time to discover what they know about their own
strengths and weaknesses under their birth signs.

By doing this, you will be better equipped to
analyze your boss, a prospective date, or help you
better understand your own child you

may have one day.

You may want to take some time and ask your parents, grandparents, aunts, and uncles questions about what they liked to do when they were children. What did they want to be when they grew up? Were they able to accomplish what they hoped for in their lives?

Doing this process will help you understand what problems they may have encountered and why they became the persons they are today. It will also give you some perspective in real time about what talents or traits you may have picked up from them unknowingly.

# TOLERANCE

# Tolerance

Tolerance represents an acceptance of another person regardless of whatever differences or interests they have in comparison to my own.

For example, they may have a different faith than mine.

They might like a different team than I do.

A person might like cats instead of dogs or birds or other animals that I might not have any desire to own or be around.

They might not have any interests as mine.

An individual might lean toward an attraction or interest in someone else, having the same sex as their own.

As long as a person doesn't try to put their beliefs, feelings or viewpoints onto mine, I have no problem showing tolerance and acceptance towards them.
We can express our differences without allowing them to interfere with activities we enjoy doing together.

# Chapter 5

## Standing Up For What's Right

While I am collecting my thoughts for this book and the love notes I want to write, another school shooting just happened in Florida. It is an overwhelming sadness I feel and so I pause to reflect on this tragedy. I have never forgotten the shootings at Sandy Hook in Connecticut.

No other country, but America, seems to keep having this problem over and over again with the politicians in office, refusing to act to keep this from ever occurring again. Australia stopped it after only one incident!

Children in America need to know they are safe from any harm, while they are attending any school or college.

In fact, *all Americans* need to feel safe when they go to a movie, fill up their gas tank, go to church, attend a concert, or whatever tasks or enjoyment they choose.

It is hard when children get a jolt, having to face the reality when these shootings occur. When I was little, I had no awareness of the world except for my own immediate family and my routine of going to school and coming home afterwards. Daily life was simpler.
I lived in a small town in upstate New York,
*Geneva on Seneca Lake.* It is a beautiful city, and

Geneva is a very friendly and peaceful community.

There was never any such violence then.

There should not be any violence now either.


Watching the news and seeing high school students

stand up in their communities throughout America and

say *'Enough!'* is so encouraging. Adults have not been

able to convince those elected into Congress to act and

make changes to gun laws. So maybe our children will

be the ones to make a difference in this terrible fight

*to stand up and finally make things right*. This story

will still be going on when my book goes to press.

I stand by any students willing to speak up and have

their voices heard.

These students are not only using their courage to act, but they are realizing that it may only take one person among them to *make a difference.*

In fact, when you act as a group, or when you act solo – *each one of you can – and will – make a difference.*

# CONVICTION

## Conviction

Conviction represents a status of a very strong belief or mindset that no one or nothing can persuade me to change.

It is a viewpoint that is grounded in strength with a bit of courage. Conviction is helping one to stand tall with their confidence or belief.

The presence of conviction is showing me the individual has the determination and the persistence to follow through on the cause or topic they are standing up for; that they will fight and stand in their conviction to make things happen.

# Chapter 6

## Living In Truth and Integrity

When I speak about your truth, I am talking about you being honest, genuine, and connected or aware of the *real* facts or truths about yourself and your life. Some children or adults may represent themselves in a phony or artificial manner because they think that's what someone wants to hear or expects from them. This example is someone who is not living in their own truth or with integrity.

The sooner you can live without censoring your own inner feelings and show the true essence of your being, the sooner you will live your genuine life. Once you start doing this, you will see things will be more aligned and work for you, like magic.

Examples of someone *not* living in their truth:

- ❖ Someone who represents themselves to be straight when they are gay or vice versa.

- ❖ Someone who represents themselves to be rich when they are poor or vice versa.

- ❖ Someone who tells others they are employed in a high level manager position when they are either unemployed or they have a lower level position or vice versa.

- ❖ Someone who pretends they are of a different faith other than the one they have.

- ❖ Someone who is not facing they are unhappy in a relationship or marriage, or someone being abused and they keep these facts hidden from their friends or relatives.

Examples of someone living in their truth:

- ❖ When you are honest about your life when talking with others.
- ❖ When you are able to express your own truth and convictions about things that matter to you.
- ❖ When you can internalize, realize, and face when you are not living in an honest and truthful reality.

As soon as you deal with the genuine facts about life,

you will be on your way to empowering yourself.

You will start to believe in who you truly are.

Being honest with yourself and others lets you 'walk

your talk' (a Native American Indian expression).

When you are living in total honesty, or being totally genuine about yourself, you are able to set an example of truth and integrity for others to follow and respect.

When you are able to totally accept the truth about what is happening in your life or with yourself, you will find things in your daily life that miraculously seem to fall into place. You will also feel more in balance and more in touch with your spiritual and natural environment.

**Remember not to follow the crowd.**

Be true to your own feelings and remain true

to the essence of you (the _I AM_ of you).

# PERCEPTION

## Perception

My interpretation of perception is an outlook or understanding of someone else's point of view about a situation.

For example, I can perceive in my analysis of someone's negative comment about a sweatshirt I am wearing that they are really saying in their criticism that they are actually saying they don't like me.

Perception is when you interpret's someone's comment or viewpoint and then you internalize the meaning to be directed towards yourself.

In actuality, the person's comments may be totally innocent and not intended to be misinterpreted in that way or have any negative meaning at all.

In using perception, a child or adult may think he comprehends a person's meaning. Sometimes misunderstandings occur because people are not comprehending what someone was trying to say.

A person who is perceptive fully understands the meaning behind an idea, a concept, or a principle without an explanation.

# Chapter 7

## Things May Not Be What They Seem

Today some children may like to play with board games while others are attracted to action games on a video type console or saber light weapons. These games or weapons all seem innocent enough, right? Today's toy manufacturers make items look very realistic and to be the genuine object.

When I was growing up, children liked to play with dolls, card and board games with family and friends or play outside with neighbors and pets. Some liked to play cowboys and Indians because television shows then focused on westerns.

It was a simpler time to grow up. We didn't have social media outlets or the internet to distract us from our play time. We also had to go to the library to look up information in reference books to help us answer questions we weren't able to find in our textbooks. To this day, I still love holding actual books.

The following information I want to share with you may already be something you have heard or learned. However, the information I am sharing is very necessary to discuss and for you to **know** inside, and be aware of every day for the rest of your life.

You must **make sure** you share the information with

your friends or siblings... and not just know

about... but **always remember no matter your age!**

If you ever see a gun on the ground or on a table, or in

a cupboard, or *anywhere* within your eyesight or within

your reach, **stop** whatever you are doing and **run** to tell

a parent or any adult that is nearby. **Do not pick up**

**the gun at anytime. Do not touch the gun at any**

**time.**

You might innocently think it's just a toy gun.

You need to remember that things are **not** always as

they seem. **Never reach for and never pick up a gun!**

Look at guns as **very** dangerous weapons that can

harm you or a friend or relative. You **never** want to take the chance of picking up a gun when it could accidentally fire without your ever pulling the trigger. You could injure or kill a beloved friend or yourself.

The statistics today are noted that guns are the **third** cause of children's deaths in America today. We can help to stop this from happening if every child pays attention and follows the **stop, run, and tell rule.**

Because I Have A Love For *All* Children, I feel it is my responsibility to inform you about gun safety because you may have been absent from school when they performed demonstrations on this topic.

Maybe you were present for them or your father or mother might have told you to be cautious, but you forgot.

*Please remember this lesson. You could save a life and especially your own!*

# EMPATHY

# Empathy

What empathy symbolizes is someone who
can relate to what another individual is feeling.
For example, if a friend of mine is crying over the
loss of their pet, I am able to have empathy for them
because I can remember what it felt like when I lost
my own dog.

Empathy is a deeper feeling than just having
compassion for someone. Empathy is an understanding
of a person who is going through a difficult
time. Someone who has empathy remembers and
relives the experience internally.

It is putting yourself in that person's shoes

because you have either been through the full

experience yourself or you have been through

a difficult time, and you can feel empathy for them.


Empathy means an opening up of your heart for

anyone having a hard time and having the ability to

understand and relate to their circumstances.

# Chapter 8

## Communication and Awareness

When you are at school you might see another student sitting alone having lunch or sitting away from everyone else.

Have you ever approached someone sitting alone in the example above and invited them to join you? Or, have you wondered why they are away from the rest of the crowd? Did you ignore this kind of situation and never give it any more thought?

Well, part of our lessons here are to learn how to communicate with clarity so that we can avoid misunderstandings.

*No one* can read what is on your mind. Unless

you *tell* someone what you are feeling or thinking,

no one will be able to communicate with you or help you.

If you are troubled by something or feel alone, please

let someone know what you are feeling, so they can

help talk about whatever problem you are facing and

can help you find a solution.

When you see someone sitting alone at school, invite

them to sit with you at lunch or play at recess with

you and your friends. No one should feel they are

isolated from the rest of the crowd.

Some schools around the country have started

implementing this philosophy.  If your school doesn't

have this, then take action now to help other students

feel welcome.

In the cases where students were thought to be

troubled, they took a gun to school to take revenge

on teachers and fellow classmates because they felt

they were ignored or they had slighted them.

Newscasters found out later that these same students

felt isolated and alone over a long period of time.

Maybe if some students had tried to befriend them

by inviting them to join their friends for lunch or

be part of their group over time, maybe these events could have been avoided by showing an act of simple kindness and consideration. We will never know.

It is something to think about and show kindness.

Opening up about what you are feeling or thinking also offers your family or friends the opportunity to communicate what they may be thinking about the same topic.

Communicating helps clear up misunderstandings that caused hurt feelings because something that was said was misinterpreted. Getting into discussions about issues that may be troubling you can clear the air and help you discover the true explanation of what was stated originally.

Having an awareness of others around you and being able to express yourself openly will give you more tools to work with as you grow older.

# Chapter 9

## Being Kind To Others

When I was a little girl, my mother was a Sunday School teacher for our synagogue. One day she asked our class a question stating, "Who was the person responsible for the golden rule *'do unto others as you would have them do unto you'*?" I raised my hand first and my mother called on me. I excitedly answered, *"Hillel"*.

It doesn't take a lot of effort to show kindness and consideration for others and to follow the golden rule. Each and every one of us is completely different from anyone else. Yet, we **all** have the same basic wants and needs no matter *where* we are living in this world.

Special Quote Related To This Topic

By

Mr. Fred Rogers (of The Mister Rogers Show):

*"You Know Things Like Friendship And Love Don't Cost Any Money At All And They Are Very Very Important."*

Remember to offer a smile as you greet someone new in your path because it may open new doors of friendship, love or even a new opportunity you never dreamed of.

As Mr. Rogers said, you can offer friendship and love *numerous times* and it doesn't cost you *anything*.

You may find in your life that some people you meet are stingy in expressing their feelings for others. Sadly, in some families, mothers or fathers do not know how to express their own feelings to their children, so they may take their frustrations out on others, not even knowing why.

You can help change the world around you by caring about everyone *else* around you.

There may come a time when someone you befriended will need to come to your rescue one day.

Some people on our planet may not care about following the golden rule at all times. They can end up disappointing us by doing or saying something hurtful or by being inconsiderate to us by the words they say.

We can move forward by forgiving them and finding other friends in our lives that have the same feelings and values we choose to follow.

One lesson, I wish someone explained to me earlier in my lifetime, is that people will come in and out of our lives as we continue to grow and reach adulthood.

In some cases, more often during adulthood, some

people will come in and out of our lives so that we can learn lessons from them and they can learn lessons from us.

Some of the friends we make will stay with us forever and there will be others who will stay only a short time – either when you have learned your lessons from each other – or when the friendship has not been a positive influence for you over a period of time.

It will help you to know that you do not have to accept another person's negative attitude or personality as your own. You can stand your ground as a thoughtful, respectful individual who shows kindness for others at all times, when they do not.

Children are often mean to their peers. Don't ever let someone's unkindness toward you become part of who you are meant to be...a kind and loving soul.

Always remember that **kindness is a conscious choice.**

# Chapter 10

## Loving And Caring For Our Planet Earth

For those of us living in The United States of America, we live in a beautiful country. There are many beautiful parks and places we can admire and visit. We have wonderful landmarks to study and appreciate. It would be a terrible day when any of these places are closed or destroyed because we didn't take the time to protect or care for them.

We can also pick up after ourselves and throw our plastic bottles in the trash instead of discarding them in our lakes or oceans. Doing something so carelessly can hurt and kill the fish and wildlife who help the eco system exist on the coral reefs and ocean floor.

I recently had the great pleasure of watching the spectacular television show, "Planet Earth-Blue Planet II" where you can visually see species of different fish maintaining their own existence. You can learn how some breeds of fish also help coral reefs grow and survive.

Taking the time to study nature and our oceans will give you a sense that we are not here alone to just exist by ourselves without any care for others or anything else. It shows us we need to connect to everything, respect and protect our planet.

# Chapter 11

## Being Kind To Animals

All animals come to us to give us their unconditional love and support at all times if we let them. They are never here to judge us or condemn us. They help us during difficult, lonely times and bring us joy.

Each animal on our planet also represents for us a sign or message we are here to learn.

In American Indian lore, animals were considered to offer us 'medicine' depending on what they symbolized. For example, a horse symbolizes 'power' where the eagle represents 'God's presence' or our connection to the Divine, or a dog represents 'loyalty'. These are beautiful symbols to read about and see which animals seem to resonate most within yourself. It can mean they are your protectors or it can mean they have come to you with a message to learn.

Each animal has a message representing lessons such as: strength, joy, courage, respect, boundaries, and many more. They visit us daily if we have the awareness to look for the messages or signs they are sending us.

There are various books on the 'medicine' animals signifying American Indian lore to use as a reference, which I will cover in another chapter.

I have come to the realization that our animals represent the overall lesson we need to express. For everyone who comes in our own individual path at all times – *acceptance and unconditional love*.

Special Quote Related To This Topic

By

Jim Henson

"In Their Own Words" – Aired PBS 3-6-18

*"Please Watch Out For Each Other And Love And Forgive Everybody. It's A Good Life. Enjoy It."*

## Chapter 12

## Growing Up Through The Cycles Of Our Lives

## With Balance And The Medicine Wheel

Throughout our growing up years, and after we reach

adulthood, we are constantly revolving through

different cycles of growth and learning experiences.

When we graduate through the lessons of one cycle

we proceed to the next step or growth cycle.

This is sometimes referred to as "the wheel of life".

In The American Indian heritage it is referred to

as "The Medicine Wheel".

Each cycle we reach and pass through teaches us a

valuable lesson. It also helps us to maintain balance and helps us become centered in place with our planet earth.

Whenever we are centered and balanced within ourselves, we feel a sense of *wholeness*. We maintain a care of our bodies and our child within – no matter what our age. We also feel younger and have a more youthful and healthier outlook throughout our lives.

In "The Medicine Wheel" folklore there is great symbolism in comparison to the cycle of our lives. The circle of the wheel is continuous and never-ending as the lessons in our lives also continue day-to-day and year-by-year ... always.

Each direction on "The Medicine Wheel" is represented by an animal. Each animal has a message such as: strength, joy, courage, respect, boundaries, and many more.

Each direction on "The Medicine Wheel" (East, West, North, or South) has an animal representing that direction and what each animal stands for. There are many variations of which animal is in each direction depending on which tribe's beliefs are being interpreted. For simplicity, I will use my reference from "*The Medicine Cards*," by Jamie Sams and David Carson. Though the authors list several tribes on their acknowledgment page, it is significant for me that they included the *Seneca* and *Iroquois*

tribes. These same tribes were known to have lived

in my hometown. I actually stood, as a child, on their

sacred burial Indian mound. It felt very special to me.

The animal in the East is the *eagle* and stands for

Great Spirit (God), and our connection to the divine.

The animal in the South is the *coyote* and represents

humor, lightness and our connection to our inner

child within. The animal in the West is the *bear* and

represents our time to be by ourselves so we can

become introspective about our lives or a situation.

We may need to give some thought in order to reflect.

The animal in the North is the *white buffalo* and represents prayer and abundance.

Since our cycles repeat in our 'circles of lessons' over time, the Indian Medicine Wheel is a good example of the continuous flow of growth in our lives. As we achieve the knowledge, understanding, or experience required, we then move on to the next direction and the next lesson. So triumph is with our own "cycles", or circles, depending on our ability to grasp our experiences. Once we graduate and learn the lesson, we move on to the next spoke in the wheel or direction. We are constantly evolving and changing as we grow, mature, and become more spiritually aware within ourselves.

As I explained earlier, (about taking the time to get to know yourself through the use of your birth sign's tools), there is a great deal to learn from our animals, as they supply us with unconditional love along with their lessons they each represent.

Regardless of which resource you use to discover your personal totem animals and the messages they bring you, please know you can call on your *own* animal guides for the assistance you need at anytime.

*For simplification, only 4 directions are touched on here. There are additional directions in the Indian lore: *Above, Below, Within, Left,* and *Right.*

Animals may also come to us at any time throughout our lives to serve as a sign. There is a lesson present for us to learn at any given moment.

Your animal awareness at an early age will hopefully help you be able to recognize them, when they appear to you in front of your very own eyes.

I wish to acknowledge that American Indians also make ceremonies to honor the four seasons in a similar ritual that Wiccan followers do to honor our

planet Earth.

# Chapter 13

## Getting In Touch With Nature

No matter what a person's religious preferences are, getting in touch with nature is truly a blessed event. Like the animals on "The Medicine Wheel," all nature has its cycles and symbols for us to learn from and feel connected.

Take time to get in touch with nature – animals – birds – plants –flowers – trees- oceans – lakes – mountains – as well as the elements of air – wind – sea – earth. They are as much a part of you as your family and friends are a part of you. Each of these has its own energy vibration, which we can connect with should we choose. American Indians honor

Mother Earth. They see and recognize the

sacredness of all things. They are able to see the

sacredness of God in our trees, plants, animals, etc.

They call on their spirit energies whenever the

need arises.

I remind you, again, to please remember to

show kindness to all animals and honor the God spirit

in *them*. As you do this small gesture, you will be

honoring the God spirit in *you*.

It only takes a moment to give or show a kind

gesture to an animal, a stranger, or someone you

know. This one small, kind gesture could be one of

the most treasured experiences that individual will remember. The principle of treating others the way you would like to be treated is always a fundamental and meaningful rule to follow.

Sensitivity and kindness to animals – since they are here to help lighten our load and share joy and love – is as important as breathing and showing kindness and compassion toward others.

Children are often mean to their peers. As I stated previously, don't ever let someone's unkindness toward you become a part of your own character. Be the kind, caring individual you were meant to be.

When I was in 8th grade, some classmates made some nasty remarks to me and about me. I don't recall what they were about exactly. What I do remember is that right after this event occurred, I went to my next class.  The teacher gave us an assignment to write an essay about any particular topic we wanted and turn it in before we left for our next class.

I had forgotten all about the essay. A year later, when I was in 9th grade, I was meeting with the school's guidance counselor because a situation had occurred I needed to report. In my session with her, she pulled out of my school records file the essay I had written.

I had titled the paper, "I will always stand up for myself". The meaning of the paper was that I would never allow anyone to put me down – not ever!
I have stood my ground my whole life. That decision gave me the strength to have my personal power developing my personality as an adult.


You can too!

# Chapter 14

## Self-Esteem Compared to an Overblown Ego

Some people may develop or grow up quicker than others. Some of us may need to learn particular life lessons at a much later time frame than our contemporaries or our friends. There is no race or time clock that we have to follow in order to learn life's lessons. When we are more developed and ready to grasp the meaning of some life lessons is when things will start to make more sense to us.

We do need to take pride in ourselves when we accomplish things such as receiving an "A" on a test or essay or when we graduate to another grade level.

These are examples of how we validate ourselves, and how we acquire our self-esteem with one achievement after another one.

Validating ourselves and honoring what we are able to accomplish at different stages of our lives is very important.

What we need to be careful of, however, is learning how to maintain a sense of humility through the processes we complete, and through each hurdle we jump.

We want to make sure we convey a sense of confidence and self-esteem without becoming an obnoxious personality with an overblown ego.

For example, there was a well-known actress in
the media recently because she had been stopped
by the police. They suspected she was driving under
the influence of alcohol.

Instead of going quietly with the police, she made
a big blow up noise by getting it featured in
the press about her being a famous actress.
**"Don't you know who I am?!"**, she huffed.

I admired this particular performer's work up until
the minute I heard about this incident.

The admiration I had toward this actress was gone. Her movies didn't make her who she is as a person. She had managed to achieve success in portraying a character in a movie that was likable. It didn't mean she became that good person's character in real life, that movie audiences cheered.

As I stated in an earlier chapter, *no one* is better than anyone else, and *no one* is above the law no matter who they are and no matter what their 'title' or 'position in life' happens to be.

It will help you to remember later on in your life when you find yourself out in the world as an employee or even as a boss of your own company:

Your job, your title or your position in life is **not who you are**! It really is *'what's inside you that counts'*.

Remember to convey to others your humility through your accomplishments in life, as well as your failures. Even when we are open to showing we are vulnerable, we are fortifying ourselves by standing in our own strength and our own power.

It is the inner core of you or your very internal essence that matters; and that others will admire through any good times or any bad. It will also help you because there may be a layoff from a job or a position that you loved and that you attached your essence to. The *job* is not who *you* are.

Being able to remember that the job you did or position you may have had was not who you *truly* are, will help you to move on to another opportunity with your own ego and self-esteem intact.

## Chapter 15

## Our Rainbow Connection With Others

Many of you may have already realized that our own individual sexual preferences are determined by the time we are three years old.

In this day and age it is sad for me to express that there are some people who hold high political stature in our country today that still think they can 'change' a person's sexual tendencies by putting them through their old-fashioned thinking with regimen and rituals.

Our identities are formed before we are ever born! *No one* outside of ourselves gets to decide that part of us! *Not ever!* It is one of the things that helps to make each of us the unique individual we are and that sets us apart from everyone else.

I am *not* a better person because I am a girl attracted to a boy, any more than another kid is better than I am because they are attracted to someone of their same sex.

Everyone has the same needs and desires to be loved and validated no matter what their sexual preferences. Everyone deserves to live in peace and happiness in accordance with *all* of our unalienable rights as stated in the Preamble of our Constitution. I can't repeat this enough because it is that important!

The diversity we have in our country is a melting pot of so many people from so many different countries and small nations that have helped us become the great nation we are.

Our ancestors arrived on the shores of The United States seeking freedom from oppression from the countries they came from, so they could have the ability to  practice their free speech without fear of persecution and to also have the freedom to practice their own religion.

Yet, today, some people in our government want to take these same rights away from us that have been preserved by law for so many years. Who is to say they won't try to pass a new law limiting our freedom to choose the partner we want in our lifetime?

We all need to be reminded of an example of one sad and shameful true story in America's history only about three decades ago.

At first there was an illness causing many men to become ill and die. No one knew what it was. Some thought it was a new and unrecognized flu and the number of people falling ill from it were astronomical.

It later came to be known as AIDS and it was thought

that only homosexual men transmitted the disease to one another. This thinking was proven wrong when heterosexual men and women were found to have also contracted the disease and some babies were even found to have contracted AIDS when they were born.

There seemed to be pandemonium in our country, and people were afraid because they didn't understand how the illness was contracted. It didn't reach the height of awareness in the public's eye until the famous celebrity, Rock Hudson, announced in a press conference that he had contracted AIDS. People were afraid to even hug a person with AIDS for fear of contracting the disease.

Rock Hudson's close friend, Elizabeth Taylor, stood by him. She formed The Elizabeth Taylor AIDS Foundation so that monies could be raised for research and a cure.

Unknown in the early stages of awareness of AIDS, people were getting blood transfusions in hospital procedures. They didn't know then that some donors who had donated their blood to blood banks had unknowingly and previously contracted AIDS. So hospitals used the blood for people in need of transfusions in order to survive their particular medical conditions.

I mention this past history because of the unique and and very brave and special individual, Ryan White.

Ryan White was only 13 years old. He was a hemophiliac and a blood transfusion he received had been tainted with AIDS causing Ryan to contract AIDS. (A hemophiliac is someone whose blood does not clot normally.)

Ryan went through a lot of persecution and fear in the school he attended. Teachers, as well as some parents, wanted him banned from attending the school. People were cruel and called him names and thought he had to be 'gay' to have AIDS. People were just plain ignorant, cruel, and mean.

It is something I hope my readers will *never* be.

Ryan White and his family moved to a different city, so that he could follow his wishes to attend school after fighting for this right in courts.

Ryan White died shortly before his own high school graduation. Congress passed legislation in his name that has helped to fund the research and care for AIDS patients in The United States.

Ryan also became friends with celebrities such as Michael Jackson. Elton John became a very close friend of Ryan's and his parents. Elton John formed

The Elton John AIDS Foundation, Elton has raised over $200 million dollars and, to this day, he is very active in his foundation after 25 years.

No child should ever go through the torment and treatment that was so shamefully hurled at Ryan White.

Ryan understood people's attitude because they lived in fear of the unknown and had a lack of understanding.

We need to set examples that we no longer treat others this way, if we have a fear about someone's lifestyle or situation.

Fear is the **only** thing we need to stop in our minds,

our actions, and our thoughts.


Take the time to ask questions to someone you

may not understand. Asking questions helps educate

yourself about people, and helps you to understand

why they do what they do or why they think or act

in a certain way.

# Chapter 16

# Awareness of Our Past History To

# Protect People

I would be remiss if I didn't address some issues and bring them to your attention in case you haven't been informed.

It is because you readers are the future leaders of America, or whatever country you happen to be from, that you need to know about some issues in case they have been overlooked or lessons were not covered or missed in school or at home.

Issue # 1:

An innocent young black boy was walking home from

a convenience store where he bought a few snacks to bring home. On his way home, some white man in a car followed him. He called the police claiming the kid had a gun. When the police told him they would handle it, the man stayed in pursuit of him. The man eventually caused an altercation to occur. He struggled with the boy and shot him as the boy was close to reaching his own home or neighborhood in Florida. The boy I am referring to was named Trayvon Martin. He did **nothing** wrong. Trayvon was only trying to defend himself! The driver in question used the excuse that because the boy was wearing a hoodie that boy needed to be stopped cold. This kind of human behavior has gone on and on and on and it has to stop! We need to be able to protect our children no matter what they

So the moral of this is *any black child's life matters*!

In fact, *all children matter to me*!

The people who do these kind of actions whether they are private citizens or the police who shoot black people in their backs claiming it was *self defense need to be held accountable, and be brought to justice.*

## Issue # 2:

American Indians were terribly mistreated by the United States Government. They were stripped of their identities, their lands were confiscated, and they were forced to move to desolate lands that were barren. They were said to be 'savages' but they were only fighting for their rights and their lands. They were outraged at how they were

plundered and so they fought back in retaliation.

There is little restitution that can ever make up for

how they were treated. There definitely needs to

be a healing here.

Issue #3:

The United States of America and its allies went to

war against Japan and then Germany (World War II).

You have probably learned in school about the attack

on Pearl Harbor in Hawaii on December 7, 1941.

What you may not be aware of, however, is that

over 10 million* *innocent* Jews and countless millions

of others were killed by the Nazis in concentration

camps in a mass genocide operation. Some countries

like Iran try to say it is a hoax and that it never

happened. Well, sadly, it is a terrible tragedy.

*Yes, the **Holocaust** did happen!* Atrocities like this

should *never* be allowed to happen ever again.

Because some states have chosen not to include

this information in history textbooks, I am telling

you about this here in order for you to be informed.


I mention this history because there are still hate

groups like the Nazi party that holds rallies in America

to try to drum up more hatred for their stagnant and

putrid philosophy. What is very interesting about this

is that Germany forbids any kind of rallies by any hate groups such as Nazis or whatever other similar groups call themselves. Why doesn't America finally comply with this same mindset? Germany has also passed laws forbidding any swastika signs defacing any building or property or from being placed anywhere in the country. (Swasticas were the sign representing the German Nazi party.) America needs to follow Germany's example to not allow the hating racist groups from having *any* voice or platform *especially* since hate crimes are classified as such in our legal court system. Present and future leaders need to pick up and solve this problem so that things like a Nazi party can never grow and fester into becoming a powerful controlling government here in America or *anywhere else* in the world.

You might be interested in reading the book,

*"The Diary of Anne Frank"*. Anne and her family

lived in Amsterdam. They went into hiding with

other families behind the offices of her father's

business so they could stay safe from the Nazi's

cruel deportations – and later revealed – to be deadly

gas chambers and concentration camps. Anne

started writing in her diary at age 13. Her entries

in the diary stopped when the Nazis stormed through

their living quarters, collected them up, and hauled

them away to the camps. Fortunately for history,

Miep Gies, one of the brave helpers who brought them

supplies and food to their hiding place, found Anne's

diary, saved it, and gave it to Anne's father, who

survived the concentration camps. Anne had dreams and wishes like everyone else, which are now revealed in her diary to readers all over the world.

In the different yet same comparison, people who stand up for the confederate flag in America don't realize that flag *stood for slavery* which was *abolished* and *outlawed* in America centuries ago. It is time we stand up together against causes that *hurt* people.

We need to *stand up for and stand by them.*

Having the freedom to speak and the freedom to write should not, in fact, mean that anyone can spue and spit out hatred for any violent cause they represent any longer.

The recent event I am referring to is the one that occurred in Charlottesville, Virginia. An innocent woman was killed at what was supposed to be a peaceful rally against confederate statues (that represent slavery to many). Things like this shouldn't happen – period!

While our democracy in The United States of America is something other nations and people admire, we still fall short in not being able to correct some unbalances like these examples I mentioned.

We have finally recognized The Reverand Martin

Luther King with a monument in his honor for his
sacrifices made in fighting for The Civil
Rights Movement.

We also have a couple new museums established for
Black History and for Civil Rights.  A new museum
just opened in Alabama signifying the racial bigotry
during slavery in several states which caused terrible
murders done by hangings to innocent black men,
women, and children.

It is my hope that you will 'pick up the torch' in a
peaceful and dignified manner, when you are of age,
and help fix areas of injustice that need to be righted,
no matter where you happen to live.

*Historically, 6 million Jews is the most quoted figure whenever the topic of the Holocaust is discussed. However, recent and up-to-date figures have been astronomically reported to be more correctly in the range of 10 million Jews killed during the Holocaust with more areas of extermination being discovered than authorities could have ever imagined. It is taking history time to correct the true number of these figures. Homosexuals as well as 'unfavorables' such as people the Nazis classified as 'invalids' or those people who opposed their actions were also sent to labor and concentration camps and were killed.

Special Quote Related To This Topic

By

Yehuda Bauer

Greatest Israeli Scholar Of The Holocaust

*"Three Commandments Have Emerged*

*From The Shadow Of The Holocaust:*

*Thou Shalt Not Be A Perpetrator*

*Thou Shalt Not Be A Victim*

*Thou Shalt Not Be A Bystander"*

# Chapter 17

## Don't Sell Yourself Short

You need to like and love yourself *first before* you can feel comfortable with others. People who end up committing to others in relationships or marriage later in life who don't know how to *like* and *know* themselves *first* will never be able to make themselves happy. Instead, they place blame on the other parties involved because they didn't understand they *first* had to feel comfortable in their own skin and *know* themselves.

You also need to like *and* love yourself and be number one for yourself at all times! That's not being selfish but not being self-sacrificing either.

You also come *first* in your feelings, your needs, and in your truth.

Don't ever be so self-sacrificing that you forget yourself and your own needs when your are helping others to fill their needs.

Please remember that you never have to feel that you have to settle for less than whatever it is you desire or feel that you deserve. Per **Anthony Robbins'** **quote, "You do not have to settle for less,"** (in a relationship), **"than you expect you deserve to be treated."**

You also need to be able to choose a profession that makes *you* happy and that you really have a passion to do. Do not choose one because you feel someone in your family or a mentor expects you to become a doctor or nurse or whatever it may be.

Do what makes you happy, what will bring you joy, what will make you feel fulfilled, and what *you* feel is *your* truth and *not* someone else's truth.

You deserve to be *who you are* and you deserve nothing but the best in whatever your feelings are, they matter first.

In honoring your feelings, you honor yourself, you honor *your truth*, you honor *your beliefs*, and you honor *your convictions*.

# PERSISTENCE

# Persistence

Persistence represents your ability to never give up. When something doesn't work out, I continue to try other ways to get my goal accomplished until I reach the finish line.

It means, for me, to continue to follow through as though I already reached my goal or achieved or acquired that job, home, item, or place in question.

It means **never** giving up until you reach the solution you were seeking.

# Chapter 18

## Recognize Your Passions

Learn what interests you have or what you feel you are good at, what passions you dream of or want for yourself. By passions, I mean, what do you feel deep in your heart and soul are your interests, dreams, or goals for yourself?

For example, when I was a child I loved to watch ballerinas dance and I wanted to be able to take ballet lessons. I watched entertainers perform in shows doing tap and jazz, and I also wanted to take tap and jazz lessons; my parents gave me the gift of these classes.

Later on, as I grew older, I recognized that acting was a talent and a stronger passion of mine.

I learned that my maternal grandmother, my mother and her siblings had been directors and performers acting in plays and musical variety shows. It was something that I felt down deep in my very own soul that I wanted to be able to accomplish.

Years later, as an adult, I was able to direct, act, sing, and dance in musical comedy theater shows as well as getting cast as a lead actor role in a play. I also received the added bonus of teaching musical comedy theater to children ages 8 through 12.

They won "special recognition awards" for their performances, and I felt very proud of them.

It is natural as you grow and mature to choose different dreams for yourself and discover new goals and passions.

Learn to believe in yourself, in your abilities, and in your dreams.

The confidence and belief in yourself, along with persistence and determination, is all that you need to succeed. These are all part of knowing and loving yourself better.

When you are able to love and understand yourself you are then able to better understand others.

When you are able to believe in yourself and you *know* in your heart you are following your passions there is *no doubt you will succeed!*

Special Quote Related To This Topic

By

Walt Disney

*"All your dreams can come true if you have the courage to pursue them."*

# PERSEVERANCE

## Perseverance

Perseverance represents someone who continues on through any struggles, conflicts, or hardships.

There is *no* stopping this person. They are mightier and stronger than they even know!

Sometimes life hands us one situation after another, and it can seem as though we are being tested because of all the trials we may have to go through.

A person who has perseverance keeps moving forward and continues on through whatever the circumstances until they are all resolved.


*This* person reaches the invisible finish line every time.

## Chapter 19

## Remember To Laugh And Lighten Up Often

## And Live With Joy

The ability to remember to "keep the child in you alive" will help sustain you throughout all of your growing cycles into and through adulthood.

Learning to play and laugh at yourself and with your friends in humorous situations always helps you to "lighten your load".

Through troubles or worries that seem to occupy your mind, take the time to sit down, relax and watch a comedy movie. (I personally enjoy laughing at a

Jerry Lewis movie.* Jerry never fails to make me laugh out loud no matter how many times I may have seen the same movie. They always, *always* help to lighten my load.) It will help you to laugh out loud and remember not to take yourself too seriously.

Problems in your life have a way of working out in time while you maintain your faith and perseverance – especially when you learn to relax and be still.

When there is something deeply troubling or perplexing, I always remember that God is the source of *all* things. In time, things will work out through the Universe, or God's Divine timing and working order.

Remembering to laugh helps you to stay young in spirit and live a longer, happier, and more productive life.

It will help you learn not to take yourself or your life too seriously so that you can enjoy your life with a healthy and balanced outlook.

Remember to take time for your 'child within' to laugh, have fun and relive your happy childhood memories as often as you can when you become an adult.

Being able to remember to stay in touch with your 'child within', especially when you reach adulthood, will help you to stay young in spirit, it will help to lighten your load and help you live a longer, happier, and more productive life so that you can enjoy your life with a healthy and balanced outlook.

You are here to share love, joy, and laughter – to learn to relax – in spite of whatever heavy load you feel you are carrying at a particular point in time.

If there is ever something seriously troubling you, please remember that things always look better when you wait for a new day to begin so you can give yourself the space and time to see things with a different point of view.

Take time for yourself in your daily, weekly,

or monthly schedules to have fun and share the

laughs with a friend. It will help you to replenish

your soul and energize yourself for a new and

brighter week ahead. It will help you to honor and

be in touch with your inner child or 'the child within'.


Special Quote Related To This Topic

By

Jerry Lewis


**"I Never Allowed The Child Within (Me)**

**To Die."**

*<u>For your viewing pleasure, I recommend</u>: Jerry Lewis

in : *"The Geisha Boy"* – ages 9 – 12

*"Who's Minding The Store"* – ages 9 – 12

*"It's Only Money"* – ages 9 – 12

*"The Nutty Professor"* – ages 12 and up


or any of *"The Colgate Comedy Shows"* starring

Jerry Lewis  and Dean Martin – for *all* ages

## Chapter 20

## The Universe And Universal Law

As we grow through our many cycles, our goals and dreams change as we ourselves change. What we wanted at age 15, we may no longer want when we are 20. When we are 30 or 40 we have a different perspective or outlook on life. We are probably into seeking new goals and new dreams and letting go of old ones.

If I had been coached and assisted in understanding the main theory that our thoughts can and do create our reality (as far as our dreams and goals for ourselves occur), I possibly would have had much more acute awareness at a younger age.

I then could have focused more easily on my dreams

to become attainable through *positive* thoughts

rather than thinking my dreams were not

attainable.

In other words, understanding that my own positive

thoughts and words could create the outcome I wanted

to achieve, and could have helped me to see they were

attainable, if I knew and was aware that they were!

Here is how the theory of believing in ourselves

and our dreams or goals works:

Believe in yourself and what you wish to achieve

without *any* doubt in your mind *knowing* and believing it is *already* yours.

The next step is to give thanks to The Universe, Father God and Mother Earth, or the Divine Power you believe in, for the success of achieving this dream or goal of yours, before it is visibly reached in reality.

Then 'let it go' and *know internally* within yourself that it is so achieved. Continue to just "be" you – and *trust* The Universe to place all in Divine working order and Divine timing that it will be so because you charted it all to be before you ever physically arrived on this planet.

It is important for you to also be aware that

The Universe, also known as Father-Mother Earth,

or the Divine Power you follow, wastes *nothing*.

**No energy is ever wasted or destroyed.**


*Everything* – every circumstance, every event –

*everything* – no matter how minute it may seem

to you – has meaning *and* a reason.

## Chapter 21

## Positive Thoughts Equal Positive Results

## And Mirror Imaging

We have more control in our destiny than you know.

Every word we speak, every thought that we think –

can – and does – create our reality.

Positive thoughts are powerful when we state with

our own belief in ourselves, that we can accomplish

(or believing we have already accomplished) the

object, or idea, that we are focused on achieving.

Negative thoughts or words spoken, do not harm

anyone else, but ourselves. Our thoughts and words

*mirror* our own very being.

If we wish to project positive outcomes for ourselves, then, we need to project positive thoughts and words.

Things that seem to 'come back to us' are our lessons reflecting the thoughts and words we have put out toward others.

When someone refers to "the mirror," it is this example about our good thoughts reflecting out with love toward everyone and everything. When we are operating in this positive focused manner things seem to open up to us and reflect back the love we projected earlier.

Any bad thoughts or wishes we project outwardly toward others seem to bounce back and return our own "image" we projected back to us.

If there have been situations or events in our lives that keep repeating, it means we never learned the lessons we were supposed to learn. So the cycle, or lesson, keeps repeating itself until we grasp the *entire* lesson. These things occur more often when we reach adulthood because we aren't always as quick to learn lessons like we did when we were children.

In addition, our thoughts and words mirror our very own *being*.

Which outcome would you rather be successful at? The positive results or the negative? Did you know that it takes less energy to be positive than it does to be negative? That's because you are projecting love out into the world with a positive and focused mindset.

Offering love in *all* of our intentions in life is effortless because it is where we came from.

People who live with a more optimistic outlook also

live longer than those who are pessimistic.

Remember, too, that smiling attracts friends – frowning doesn't. Try to take time to ask yourself, "What can I change about my thoughts to get the outcome I desire?" "What can I improve about myself?" Try doing this *instead* of criticizing or complaining about others.

Special Quote Related To This Topic

By

James M.Barrie's 'Peter Pan'

**"Think Lovely Thoughts"**

## Chapter 22

## Vulnerability And Sensitivity Allowance

We are all separate individuals with our own unique path and goals, yet we *all* come from the same Divine Source.

I mentioned earlier that *showing* our vulnerability and sensitivity at times actually gives us our strength.

In the past, parents raised boys to be tough and macho.

They told them 'never show your emotions or cry in front of others'.

In other words, they suppressed their sons from developing into balanced, strong, caring, and vulnerable human beings like everyone else.

When these same boys later grew up, they didn't know how to relate to their friends or wives and they didn't know how to express openly or show their emotions. Because they had been so stifled in their own life, they couldn't relate to those closest to them who were able to express themselves openly.

That was and is the *wrong* way to treat and raise boys.

We all have emotional moments in our lives when it is necessary to have these down times. If we didn't have days like this, we wouldn't recognize the joy when it happens. It is part of the balance we learn in our lives.

Allowing children to be sensitive about whatever issues or situations they face helps them develop into well-balanced children and adults.

Sad times, when a family member or a pet passes away and dies is time to cry and be sad.
No matter what the reason for the sadness, cry openly when you need to cry! There is nothing to be ashamed about when you do this.

Holding in our emotions – whether boys or girls –

is not a healthy way to approach life situations.

Boys and men should feel free to show their vulnerability and let those closest to them comfort them. There is strength in recognizing you have emotions, and you are a real honest-to-goodness human being!

On a similar outlook, children should be permitted to play with toys no matter what their particular gender happens to be. If they have creative leanings, such as becoming a clothes designer, or they show an interest in playing baseball, they should be allowed to express themselves according to their passions.

Fortunately, many parents of this century have learned to be more accepting and more respectful of their children's individuality and passions.

There are some children who are born as either a boy or girl *who know internally* they are meant to be the opposite gender. They feel differently and they are not happy in their own skin. They want to wear skirts instead of pants. Or a boy may want to wear something frilly that girls would wear.

This is called transgender and is more recognized and better tolerated by society as a whole now. Some people who are transgender have had years of self-inflicted torture and unhappiness because they felt they had to hide their true identity behind their bodies at birth.

Some children are happy with the gender they have, but they want to express themselves with funky clothes or outlandish get ups when they go to school.

Whatever your reasons or situations, if you happen to be someone who feels you are misunderstood, rejected or stifled at home or at school, please let someone know, so they can help you get this problem corrected in your life sooner rather than later.

## Chapter 23

## Children Who May Appear Different From You

Sometimes a classroom will have some children who need more personal attention from the teacher than you do.

One child may be required, due to health reasons, to be seated in a wheelchair. Another child may have a different health condition and be required to wear an oxygen pack so that he can breathe properly. There may be another child who limps, or stutters, or one who has only one arm or use of one hand.

These are examples of children who are very bright

and intelligent, but their bodies were made by The Universe or the Divine power to be different than yours.

Because some children may appear to be in a more vulnerable physical condition than others in a classroom, teachers tend to treat them as though they can't learn, think, or reason as well as other children. This is a fallacy and causes children or even adults to be evaluated incorrectly.

We plan our whole chart before we are born as to what our physical characteristics will be, who are family and friends will be, what lessons we have chosen to learn here, and what lessons we are here to give to others once we are on this planet.

People given the physical characteristics I described earlier have chosen these because they offer examples of courage, strength, and determination for us to follow.

They placed themselves in our paths to test us on our kindness, compassion, and understanding.

*Nothing* that happens in our lives is a coincidence. Things *do* happen for a *particular* reason or lesson.

## Chapter 24

## Bullying Has To Be Stopped Cold

The topic of bullying cannot be swept under a rug in a passing comment. It cannot be ignored by our society any longer. It must be addressed on *all levels* and *stopped cold*!

What I mean by *all levels* is at home, at school, in public places, social media, by the police, by cities and towns, by state legislation. Federal legislation must be passed to *outlaw any* and *all* actions and any and *all* forms and levels of bullying.

*Bullies have no power!* Just because someone calls

you a name *doesn't make it so* – or true.

Bullies have *no* place in society! None!

Anytime you feel taunted, embarrassed, threatened or harassed by someone *report it immediately.*

Sometimes bullies use peer pressure in school to make someone in school do something to someone they wouldn't ordinarily do because it isn't in their own sweet character. Don't allow any bully to force you to be mean to someone else. Instead, *report them!* Call them out for what they are. You will feel proud you did.

Authorities need to stand up in defiance of all threats or tauntings made and make the bullies pay for their actions. Innocent children or teenagers need to feel free to speak up and stand up for themselves and be supported by everyone.

There *is* a solution to bullying. It is time we no longer have to report about hundreds of children who committed suicide because they were too ashamed or afraid to speak up causing them to end up feeling so hopeless or desperate.

If you are being tracked or followed in person or on social media, *report it*! If it happens on a social media site, *stay off the site!* Your *real* friends are the ones you can see face to face and are people you actually know.

Don't share personal information about your life to anyone who can read it openly on the internet.

Keep your information private and not public for others to be free to follow you. There are privacy settings that are available.  If you have friends in your personal circle bullying you, then they are *not your friends,* and you need to rid yourself of them from your life.

Special Quote Related To This Topic

By

Mahatma Gandhi

*"You Must Be The Change You Wish*

*To See In The World"*

# Chapter 25

## Honor Your Feelings And Your Intuition

I want you to know that it is okay for you to honor your feelings. Feelings are very real, and it is okay for you to feel whatever you are thinking or feeling.

Our feelings are what give us a clue or indication of what we are experiencing. We also have what we call our sense of intuition.

Our intuition helps us sense or pick up on things that may not feel right to us even when we don't understand the reason why we are feeling a certain way.

Feelings are our barometer. They are our way of

measuring what feels good, uncomfortable, uneasy,

afraid, angry, jealous, happy, sad, stressful, etc.,

to us. Children, as well as adults, would be more

kind to themselves if they would stop for a

few minutes and just listen to their own thoughts.

It is good to ponder over what we are feeling and

analyze why we are feeling that way? What is the

cause of our doubts, our anxiety, or our fears?

Is it also your intuition giving you a warning not to

do something? Why is it giving you that warning?

Paying closer attention to our own feelings helps

us to know ourselves better and gives us the

strength to be able to communicate with our
parents, teachers, family, and friends what it is
that we believe in, what makes us "tick" and
so forth.

Don't be afraid to trust your instincts. They help
guide us through our path in life.

Do you also know you have rights? You have the same
rights as adults. A child has every right to express
him or herself. It is time for children to be able to say
what they feel or think without fear of being ridiculed
or punished for expressing themselves. (I am _not_
talking about "brattiness".)

Even though my mother and father allowed me to speak out and express my feelings when I was growing up, I experienced having the affects of almost an ulcer when I was twelve-years-old because I kept things that were troubling me inside. I did not express them openly. It took a physical ailment to show the stress that I was experiencing.
I learned from this experience that I didn't have to keep things to myself. You don't have to either.

Ask yourself, "Why do I feel this way?" What is it I am feeling or thinking and why? What is the true cause of my feelings? Are my thoughts real or are they imagined? What can I do to communicate the things that are troubling me or that I need to express out loud so that I will feel better?

I know that I always feel better when I have had an opportunity to express what I've been feeling or thinking, and I can get it off my chest.

Listen to your intuition when your inner feelings tell you, "No, that doesn't feel right. I shouldn't go with my friend to the mall or game today. It's best if I stay home." No matter how small the feeling or intuition please try to *listen* to yourself. The thoughts are there to help guide us and to help protect us in our daily lives. Walking with awareness of your surroundings is always helpful.

For example, when I was six-years-old, I was walking home from school one day when I noticed a man in a trench coat. He was standing by a car with one of the doors wide open. He was calling me and holding

a piece of candy up in the air so I could see it to

try to entice me to walk over to him. My intuition,

or my inner sense, warned me *not* to go toward

this man. It warned me to run as fast as I could.

I crossed to the opposite side of the street. When

I reached home safely, I told my mother about the

incident. She reported it to the proper authorities.

I sensed danger and honored my feelings.


In another example, as an adult, I planned to attend

a theatrical job audition with a friend one day.

The weather was terribly stormy and the rains were

coming down very strong. I felt in the long run that

it wouldn't work out for me to go. I decided to

stay home and not join my friend after all.

My friend later informed me that what we had hoped

for in the audition never took place. In addition,

she had been delayed for hours in traffic. My feelings

protected me by sensing it wasn't for my highest

good. I was glad I was able to listen and honor them.

I didn't feel pressured into doing something I didn't

feel right about.


Please know that your ability to talk about your

feelings and communicate them to others will help

you get through these growing up years. It will

help you to honor yourself which is one of the most

important things a person can do for himself.

You will then have use of these tools when you

reach adulthood. If I had been taught early on to

become more aware of trusting my instincts,

intuition, and my thoughts, I would have avoided

many setbacks I have experienced. This is one

lesson I hope you will retain for yourself and for

any of your friends or siblings, who will listen.


If no one is there to talk to you or listen at that

moment, then get a pencil and paper and write

down what it is that you would say out loud.

The idea is to get things off your chest so that

they are no longer bottled up inside of you.

Being rid of these thoughts helps our bodies to

remain more grounded and at ease with both

ourselves, those around us, or our circumstances.

We become freer because we have released any

negative thoughts...even good thoughts need to

be released or communicated. It helps us express

our love or appreciation whenever possible.

Honor the hurt, anger, or fear you feel, as well as

the joy you feel.

As part of our learning cycle, we are really here to

learn to love ourselves, one another, our planet

earth, and all its inhabitants, animals, and creatures.

What I wish for and desire is pretty much the same

as you, or your neighbor or closest friends'

desires. Though our physical appearances differ,

our overall hopes and wishes are really the same.

We all want and desire the same things in life –

to love and be loved – it is that simple. It is what

we are here to do – to honor the *I AM* in each other.

Recognizing the importance of love is one of the most valuable lessons children can possess. Learning this early in life will make you a richer person spiritually, mentally, physically, and emotionally. It will help you to be more balanced in the recognition that we are all somehow "related" spiritually.

We all have the Universe or the Divine power's unconditional loving spirit within us.

# Chapter 26

## Giving And Sharing Respect

It goes hand-in-hand that if a child is shown respect, the child will give respect back. Adults who are demanding or controlling of their children need to acknowledge that *no one owes them respect.* Children need to know that respect is *earned and deserved; it is never owed automatically.*

If a parent, teacher, relative or any adult talks down to a child, then how can that child "talk up" to them? How can children respect them? Children have just as much right to being treated with respect as adults.

Please remember that your personal self-esteem
equals the respect you also have for yourself.

Children can and need to respect boundaries of
space and privacy. However, a child's own space
and boundaries also deserve respect.

Trust the *I AM* about you.

# Chapter 27

## Our Evaluations Follow Us

When we attended kindergarten we were given

expectations we had to follow in class.

We were taught to respect and get along with each

other, to listen to the teacher, and follow the

teacher's requests while in the classroom.

When we received our quarterly report cards we

were evaluated with check marks on how well we did.

- ❖ "Gets along with others"
- ❖ "Works by herself / himself for a while"
- ❖ "Is polite and asks for permissions or excuses"
- ❖ "Offers to help another classmate"
- ❖ "Volunteers to do extra work on projects"

These are some examples of our kindergarten evaluations.

You can imagine my surprise when many years later one of my employers used these *same* simple listings to evaluate my job performance when I was already a fully developed adult!

Our records follow us *everywhere*.

By being an upstanding student and citizen, we can rest assured that we will continue to grow as an individual and as a responsible person.

## Chapter 28

## Positive Reinforcements For Children

For over forty-five years I have been knitting
baby blankets for my family's and friends' new
arrivals. Many times I have accompanied these
blankets with cards for the parents and notes telling
all babies these blankets are meant to "welcome you
to this planet and to envelop you with warmth
and love, while you are in the protection of your
loving parents and family".

I believe *all* children on this planet need to hear
they are loved and welcome!

You need to hear you are your *own unique* and *special* person.

You have chosen your *own* particular path to follow.

As you develop and learn new lessons in life, they will lead you to that path. There are no right or wrong answers as it's whatever you have chosen for your *own* soul to learn and experience.

I know you will continue to grow into the spectacular loving and brilliant human being I already know you are!

# Chapter 29

## Metaphysical Lessons

The following are a few metaphysical lessons that may help you achieve some positive results:

### Love Energy

Send love energy to those you love, as well as to those who may have hurt you or who you feel may not like or respect you. You will feel a difference almost immediately.

### Attitude

If you don't like the way things are working out with a project or whatever your focus is on, change the way you think about it. Also, walking away from it for a bit and coming back to it will give you a new outlook. A change in your attitude or thoughts can help you achieve success.

## Animal Energy

An animal's energy can be called upon to help empower you during situations you face. For example, during a dark night driving home at night, I call on owl to help illuminate the rodeway so that I can see better. Since owls have the ability to see in the dark, this is a perfect animal for me to call upon when I need this illumination. They never fail me. It is also helpful to know what each power animal's strengths are as referred to in an earlier chapter.

## Money Energy

When we are able to master the amount of energy

we use sparingly, we are also able to better understand

that money is also energy. The more we can conserve

our money energy the faster it will grow.


## Energy Projection

Before you start out for the day, send out your

love and harmony energy projections to where you are

going. If it's to school, a store, a library – wherever –

send out loving energy to all those places before

you ever arrive. You will find many times

people there will be in good harmony with you, and

things will fall into place like magic. Synergistic

things seem to happen out of the blue.

## Staying Focused In The Present Moment

When we are able to stay focused in present time on any given day, we are better able to cope with what is happening in our lives in that moment. Worrying about the future never accomplishes anything, but keeping us back from having a good day. Staying in the present is the key to feeling happier and having less stress in our lives.

# COMPASSION

## Compassion

Compassion represents an opening up of a person's heart towards another person due to an event that has happened.

Compassion is something instantaneously felt after a jolt of hearing sudden news about tragic events of a shooting, a flood, or smaller events such as a personal loss of a friend's pet or family member.

For me, compassion is something felt by humanity standing up as a whole community at times when a show of love and support is all we can give.

# Chapter 30

## Recap

You have learned to believe in yourself more now. Hopefully, I have given you more tools you can use to help you become the change we need on our planet.

Each chapter has started a foundation for you to build upon reinforcing your self-esteem and self-love.

Now that you have begun this empowering process, you also need to realize that you are the *peacemakers* of tomorrow. Allow yourself to review each topic over and over again to help empower yourself for the future of your role as a peacemaker.

It is important for you to know that whatever you end up remembering about your childhood, you are not alone in your experience. Others have had things happen to them – good and bad memories. Experiences happen for our growth. For whatever reason, we chose, before we were born, to learn from these experiences. Whether we learn to assist and prevent others from having these same experiences, to treat everyone well, to overcome great hurdles, or to set examples for others in similar situations, we see that things can be worked out. All things happen in Divine timing.

Please remember that you have tremendous resources within yourself, and you can call upon them anytime.

I want to share with you one young girl's story that was in the news recently.

A twelve-year-old girl by the name of Meghan Markle was watching a commercial  about dish soap. Meghan didn't like the way the message was conveyed as being a product implied *only* for women to use when they washed dishes. Meghan wrote a letter to Proctor and Gamble and to a newscaster where she was interviewed about it. Boys in her class had made fun after viewing the commercial and said, "See, that's all you're good for...that's what girls do".* So Meghan asked them to give a better statement in the commercial for *all* people to use it...and they did!

Meghan grew up in California and became an activist for women's equality issues. In addition, she also became a talented actress. Meghan, who played princess as a child, became engaged to Prince Harry of England November 2017 and they married on May 19, 2018. They are now The Duke and Duchess of Sussex.

This is one example of how *you can make a difference* here for everyone on this planet.

*Aired on CBS "Meghan Markle" on 4/20/18

## Chapter 31

## Music Is The Universal Language Of Our Souls

Music is the universal language of our souls. We don't need to know the words as each melody resonates inside of us and moves us deeply within our own soul.

When we hear about tragic events in the news, our souls suddenly resonate with compassion for everyone involved. We don't happen to know them. We may not even speak the same language. Our souls just know we have a sudden feeling of caring and compassion.

We need to remember that our souls are internally connected *universally*. We don't need to speak the same language or think the same way, but we are *all* connected.

It will help mankind if we can all remember our souls resonate to one another as a compassionate and loving *community always.*

I sincerely hope these *love notes* have helped to make a difference in your life.

*I Love You!*
*Wendy*

## Index Of Vocabulary Words

I chose these limited, but powerful words because
I believe these words are instrumental guides
that follow us throughout our entire lives.

## Special Recognition

I am very grateful to Victoria Vinton for her beautiful artwork on the cover. Through the process of creating my design, Victoria understood the message that I wanted to convey perfectly. She truly is an extraordinary artist!

I wish to extend my appreciation to Molly McCandless for working with me to help me acknowledge my insight into being able to write this book. Working with Molly has been, what I call, my "yoga for the soul" transformation.

Special Quote To Keep In Mind

By

George Washington Carver

*"When You Do The Common Things*

*In An Uncommon Way,*

*You Will Command The Attention*

*Of The World."*

Remembering Mattie Stepanek

Mattie's illuminating heartsongs books of poetry

were insightful beyond his

chronological years.

His gift of wisdom, love, peace, and spirituality

will live on through eternity.

Mattie,

you will forever be a

sainted and blessed peacemaker

for children and humanity.

Your presence here on this planet is greatly missed.

Books By Mattie Stepanek:

*"Heartsongs"*

*"Hope Through Heartsongs"*

*"Celebrate Through Heartsongs"*

*"Loving Through Heartsongs"*

Special Quote By Maya Anjelou

"I've learned

that people will forget

what you said, people will forget

what you did,

but people will never forget

how you made them feel."

www.ingramcontent.com/pod-product-compliance
Lightning Source LLC
Chambersburg PA
CBHW052000090426
42741CB00008B/1474

*9780692121757*